THE GREAT MAN HUNT

*Access and Attract that Guy Every
Woman Wants Using the Dating Apps*

By

Gina Hendrix

The Great Man Hunt

© 2021 Gina Hendrix

TABLE OF CONTENTS

INTRODUCTION

Hey ladies! I'm so excited that you're ready and willing to do what it takes to access the type of men you've always wanted to meet and date.

This tells me you're at a place in life where you will try something new to find, meet and date high-quality men. You know, the guy EVERY woman wants, the guy fairy tales are written about, the guy in your favorite rom-com, and the Jason Momoa of your dreams.

The number one reason women connect with me is that they want access to a great man with an exciting life who will love them like no other.

While many matchmakers and relationship experts are in the business of selling HOPE, my business is all about ACCESS. Because hope, by itself, won't get you very far.

So, I've given women access to my successful eligible clients through my matchmaking service (if and only if it's the right match) or as I'm doing here, guiding you so that you can gain access to the very best men using the dating apps on your own. Remember, access is everything, but even ACCESS isn't enough if you show up unprepared.

Let me guess:

I doubt you're new to online dating or dating apps.

Right?

My guess is that you don't believe there are any great men on the dating apps, or you are exhausted trying to find them.

1. You're the queen of attracting ALL the creeps as if you're holding a welcome sign.

2. You have a love-hate relationship with online dating apps. One day you're excited and hopeful with all the matches you're making; the next day, you're sick of seeing those faces and done with the apps. And POOF, you've deleted the app off your phone.

Either way, you're in the right place. And here's the good news, there are great men (men you want to meet) on dating apps. I promise! I will tell you exactly how to find the very best men you want to meet using them.

I'm Gina Hendrix, a relationship expert, published author, and billionaires' matchmaker with over a decade of experience helping the most eligible bachelors find their one-of-a-kind partner and helping women step-up their game to attract these types of men. You may have even seen me on Entertainment Tonight or E! sharing my thoughts about celebrity relationships.

Let's say I've learned a thing or two about how men think, what they are looking for, and what it takes for them to put a ring on it. Not to mention, I'm great at spotting the men that look the part, but who will end up wasting your time and breaking your heart.

Oh, and by the way, before I started my matchmaking business, I was one of Hollywood's top celebrity stylists. Movie stars and rock stars hired me to make sure they looked their best for photoshoots and public appearances. So, I know how to fine-tune your look from a stylist's perspective; and I know what will attract the men you want and make you stand out from the crowd.

P.S. It's not what you think.

I'm not here to tell you what you want to hear or placate you in any way. I take my job seriously when it comes to giving authentic advice and matchmaking. This is why I'm different from most relationship experts and the advice they give. I'm not going to provide you with false hope, recommend any of that hippie-dippy call him in, teach you how to get your ex back, or any of that other useless old uninspiring nonsense.

I've developed strategies that help women like you get access to the very best men based on a combination of things that I will lay out for you in this book.

First, you have to know your audience and catch their attention. Consider this your very own Great Man Hunt Road Map to gain access to A-Game, high-quality men.

Get ready, ladies; you are training for the dating Olympics. Because dating these days, is that competitive. I'm going to show you what I've learned from working behind the scenes as a personal matchmaker to the most eligible men in the world. The knowledge I share in this book will help you turn up the heat on your love life, turn your profile into a magnet for high-quality men, get clear on what you want, how to spot the creeps, and stop wasting time on 'no effort' men.

Listen, I don't believe in beating around the bush, and my honest to a fault approach isn't everyone's cup of tea. I get it! But I know if you can't be honest with someone, you can't help them. My approach has a 99% success rate, so I know it works.

But first, let me share with you one of my very favorite stories ever!

Audri was in her 60s when she first reached out to me. She was frustrated, sad, lonely, and losing hope very quickly. Over the years, she would email me with questions and tell me about her disappointment with the dating apps.

Finally, after years of this, she decided to invest in her love life and future to try something new and join my program.

Immediately, I went in and changed her photos and profile information. The images she was using did not elevate her to a level where she could attract the type of man she wanted. Bad lighting, bad angles, and her outfits, oh my.

The thing is, it didn't take much to fix all of that quickly. Audri wanted a man looking to get married who loved animals, boating, dancing, and I gave her clever ways to include all that in her profile. All of those years she spent frustrated with dating apps, and it took me no time to fix what was one of the biggest reasons she wasn't attracting Mr. Right.

And she did. Out of the gate, it made a massive difference in attracting a better caliber type of man. She then got excited, was happier, and her outlook changed. She became confident and UNSTOPPABLE!

I told her what to say during the messaging phase, how to say it, what men she needed to focus on, and she started getting better dates.

The change was immediate, and even I was as giddy as a schoolgirl. She would send me text messages here and there. Oh, and remember I said she loved boating, so we focused on drawing in those types of men.

She started dating some great men, and some didn't work out. One of the guys she liked and met on a dating app was the head of a movie studio (yes, I said the head of a movie studio); they dated for a while, but ultimately, it ended. She continued to date, and I hadn't heard from her in a long time.

Then the other day...WHAT A MAGICAL DAY...I get this text from her.

I got engaged and we are planning a wedding around New Years in key west Florida
Here's some pictures and our website of the boat we bought

I also moved to Orlando Florida and we are relocating to Sarasota next year

So thanks to you I got the man I've been searching for
Much thanks Gina !

Wow!!!! OMG Audri!!! Are you kidding me?!?! that is beyond fantastic news 😭😭😭

BUT WAIT...let me tell you the best part of this story. Audri had never been married before. Honestly, I still get goosebumps as I share the story now. She got the dream life and the man she wanted. And they didn't wait until New Years', they got married in October during COVID, and I watched via Zoom.

This could be you, should be you!

You're probably thinking, "Okay, Gina, I'm all ears....what now?"

Well, for starters, we're going to flip the script on what the guys are doing to you ladies on dating apps, and I'm going to teach you how to do that. This is where you'll be able to separate the men from the boys easily. Then you're really in a position to attract the very best. But first, let's go over how to use the guide.

How to use the guide and apply the strategies:

1. Get in a Positive Mindset

If you think there are no good guys out there, then you'll never find them. If you are in a negative place and refuse to be open-minded to new ways of doing things, you will continue to be frustrated.

You'll see what you want to see, and you will experience what you expect to experience. That's the way life works. What shows up in front of us is truly a reflection of what is in our subconscious.

And here is the perfect example. I love animals. I have a house full, and as I'm driving along, from time to time, I'll see a dog running loose by itself that has escaped from somewhere. Every time this happens, I immediately hit the brakes, pull over and help.

I have friends that say to me, "Gina, I never see any dogs running loose. How do you always see them?" And I say, "It's because that's what's in my subconscious. I'm always on the lookout." So, we see and notice what is important to us and planted in our minds. If you expect only to see creeps, you will only see creeps. If you believe there are great guys out there waiting to meet you, they will start showing up. Especially if you utilize the strategies, I am about to share with you here.

2. 30-Day Commitment

I hate to break it to you, but if you want to ditch the 'no effort' men, you first have to put in your own effort. But before you scream in agony at the thought of investing tons of time on dating sites, let me say that's the beauty of this new approach. It will make life so much easier for you.

So, no excuses, ladies! The strategies won't work if you only commit to trying them once (or twice). If you want to see results, you need to commit to these strategies for at least 30 days. Even if you get mad at me and think I've lost my mind with this advice, or you feel anxious or weird. Trust me. I've got you!

It's normal to be nervous to try these out-of-the-box strategies. And I'll warn you; they are different from what you're used to doing. But if you want different results, you have to be willing to try different approaches. This approach works for attracting the type of men you want to meet and brings them out of the woodwork.

3.You Must Be Fearless

Being fearless will come in handy because what I'm asking you to try will scare you (might scare the hell out of you). At some point, you're likely going to think (or maybe even say), "What is Gina asking me to do? I can't do that." It's most likely going to happen after I teach you my signature move: swipe like a guy. It's part of flipping the script on these guys. And I get it. These techniques aren't what you're used to doing.

But that's the point. The techniques are an experiment, and it's all safe and legal. So, don't go freaking out. It's not the end of the world. Nobody's going to harvest your organs or get mad at you. Your fearlessness is going to teach men to grow up and how to step up. So I'm asking you to stay open to learning and applying these strategies. They are going to feel weird and uncomfortable at times, but hang with me.

This guide aims to teach you things that you haven't yet tried or considered trying. If you did, you wouldn't be looking for advice. So, stay open, and trust the process. Be fearless. Be ready for change.

4. Pace Yourself

Don't go poppin' a bottle of champagne the minute one of these strategies works. I see this so often. You update your profile pics, and bam, you think better men start swiping. And before you know it, you feel like you've got this mastered, so you stop following the rest of the strategies. But here's the thing, there is more to landing your dream guy than updating your profile photos or spotting the creeps.

When things start to work, don't go off the deep end, and stick to ALL of the guide's strategies.

5. Have Fun With It

Make sure you're having fun with it. Make it a game if you want. Be playful. Trust me, ladies, men don't take this as seriously as you do (not in the very beginning). So do what you can to take the pressure off yourself. If that means swiping with friends over wine or binge-watching Netflix, that's cool. Find what works for you to make this fun.

And trust me, men are using it as a game too. I know this from my dating app and working behind the scenes. So don't take this too seriously at the initial swiping stage. Because the men aren't, I promise.

6. Ask Me Questions

As you apply the strategies, I'd love to hear how they are working for you. To get more access to me while surrounded by other fearless women at all stages of their lives, please join The Great Man Hunt group on Facebook, where I'm always sharing content, tips, and tricks for you ladies.

Ok, why wait another second.

Let The Great Man Hunt begin…

CHAPTER I

DATING APP MISTAKES
MOST WOMEN MAKE

I Know You Do This

The first step to accessing these eligible bachelors is identifying and acknowledging some of the most common mistakes I see women make on their profiles, whether they fill it out in my private database or on dating apps. And if you are making any of these, now is the time to change it up.

1. Love-Hate Relationship with Dating Apps (Negative Mindset, No Strategy)

Raise your hand if you have a love-hate relationship with dating apps?

Meaning one minute you can't get enough of them, and the next, you've deleted the apps off of your phone, and you're ready to swear off men for eternity. Well, consider this your biggest mistake. Most of the women I talk to feel this way about dating apps. They get their hopes up each time they make a match but soon realize the guy is a creep or a complete dud. They end up frustrated because they can't figure out how to make the stupid apps work (i.e., find a good man).

And they start to think, maybe something is wrong with them, or the apps are full of losers. You know the old saying, "All the good men are taken!"

I get emails like this one all the time:

Hi Gina—I'm in San Francisco. Please let me know when you do an event. I am a smart woman who's established and sophisticated and interesting, and I'm looking for a real relationship. I refuse to use dating apps. There are no men on dating apps at my level, and I know you work with the best. I would love your help.

Here's the thing, limiting your options by limiting your mindset about where they may or may not be—is not smart.

I know firsthand that good-looking, successful, high-quality men use dating apps. If you're going to learn anything from me, you have to change your mindset on this issue. And for those of you who care about this, yes, there are even Ivy-league educated men with private planes on these apps looking for serious quality relationships with women of all ages.

The woman above who wrote to me, I would guess that her pictures aren't as great as they could be, she has no clue how to spot the best ones, and she's not using a proper strategy.

All of these things add up to creating a mindset that puts her in a negative place. Once you are stuck in a negative place, unless you are determined or have someone helping you, it isn't easy to change that mindset.

Let's face it, everybody these days are on dating apps, especially since COVID-19. So if you get nothing else from what you read here, please let me reset your mind on this belief that no good men are on the apps. As it stands right now, you might not be attracting them, but they are there if you're single and looking for a relationship. You have to be open-minded and determined on dating apps. You also have to bring your A-Game. But we'll dive into that next level access a bit later.

Honestly, the app isn't working for you, probably because you aren't using a strategy that attracts this caliber of guy. And I am not talking about creating a profile, swiping right on all the cute guys, and hoping and praying Mr. Right falls into your lap. Nope, sister, that isn't the way it happens.

I'm talking about using a proven strategy and skill set that works—like the ones I will show you. So ladies, if you have a love-hate relationship with dating apps, it likely means you're approaching this with a poor mindset, or your strategy is flawed, or you're guilty of both.

2. Your Profile Doesn't Stand Out

I hate to break it to you, but the second biggest mistake I see women make on dating apps is creating a profile that doesn't stand out from the crowd in a way that attracts high-caliber men. If you have a generic profile and put little to no effort into it, then all you'll get is generic men in return.

You have to stand out from the other women that he swiped on before and after you. This is the superhighway of dating. I've reviewed 1000s of profiles during my matchmaking career, and over and over again, it all begins and ends with your photos.

It's shocking to me how many people make the same photo mistakes. You'd think I'd seen it all at this point, but I am still surprised at some of the photos I come across.

I don't say this to shame you or make you feel bad, ladies. You're going to make these mistakes if no one is candid with you. They don't want to hurt your feelings, friends don't know what men need and want to see in a photo, or you aren't taught an effective strategy.

That is why having an outside perspective and a proven strategy is a game-changer.

The biggest mistakes I see with photos are:

- Far away photos
- Filtered photos
- Not smiling
- Old photos
- Sunglasses
- Hats
- Bad outfits
- Unflattering angles
- Bad lighting
- Too racy
- Group photos

And, of course, posting an entire album of photos. It's unnecessary.

Here is something essential to keep in mind: if you have one awful or so/so photo amongst ten good ones, the not-so-great one will overrule others. Men don't want to sift through all of your photos, trying to figure out which one is the one you 'really' look like today. So when he sees one that isn't as flattering—he believes THAT is what you look like, and he's out of there—skid marks in the parking lot.

Listen up. These men put a story together about you in their minds based on your photos. When they look at your photos, these things are running through their minds:

"Sexy, I'd love to get her in bed."
"Man, two of these women are hot, but which one is she?"
"She'd be great to take to Vegas for the weekend (and that's about it)."
"Who's that guy next to her, an ex or unfinished business?"

If these things go through their heads, they won't swipe right, or they'll swipe right for the wrong reasons.

We don't want those scenarios to happen. We want the right guys swiping right and the creeps that send di*k pics to send them to someone else.

Part of my unique strategy is sharing with you how to set up the perfect profile that becomes a magnet for the 'right' guys and repellent for the losers or, at the very least, the ones who will waste your time. Because your success on the app starts with your photos, and then your profile seals the deal.

When it comes to the information you write about yourself, do not be afraid to put exactly what you're looking for on your profile. A common mistake women make is not asking for what they want. They are scared to turn anyone off and feel like they need to attract everyone. No, you don't! That's what's cluttering up your inbox and why you end up feeling overwhelmed, disappointed and hating the dating apps.

3. Swiping Only on the Cutest Guy

Another big mistake I see women make is using the hotness factor as their strategy to pick men. I mean, let's be serious; who doesn't love looking at a hot guy? Let alone making out with one. I often dream of Jason Mamoa! Who doesn't?

So it's easy to swipe right when we see a guy…

- He was flaunting his abs during a beach workout.
- He looks like Tarzan of the jungle.
- He is showing off his bright white teeth with an irresistible smile while petting a puppy.
- He is staring right through you with his piercing blue, green, or brown eyes.

You know what I'm talking about, right?

We've all seen those profile pics that take our breath away. And we catch ourselves saying to our girlfriends, "OMG, I think I've found THE ONE."

Well, this guy knows his effect on women. You aren't the only woman who thinks he's THE ONE. And since he knows it, if he isn't a good guy, he will use his magical powers to his advantage.

So ladies, hear me out. Looking for the hottest guy will leave you frustrated. And it will get you nowhere fast. As I said, that guy knows he's damn hot and can use that to his advantage.

Do you want to be one in a long line of horny ladies giving these hot men tons of options to be their plaything? Maybe. Ha. But I'm trying to help you make better choices for the long term.

Let's say the competition is high.

I've seen it time and time again where women invest so much of their energy into finding these hot guys that they get blinded by their looks and forget everything they want in a man. They settle for the crumbs he gives because he's hot. But hopefully, by now, you're too smart for that.

Eventually, it doesn't work out, or they end up miserable. Now I'm not saying being attracted to a guy isn't essential. There needs to be chemistry and attraction for sure. But just because he's the hottest guy doesn't mean he's a quality man. And I think this is something women get swayed by over and over.

While there is always an exception to the rule, there is a better chance that the hot guy you're swiping right on is going to waste your time. Please don't get mad at me. I'm just the messenger. So it's better to hedge your bet towards a better strategy, which I share below.

4. Accepting Crumbs from Bums

Okay, most of us have invested time in guys that are total bums. Maybe not literal bums, but you know what I mean. This happens because women make the mistake of not pre-qualifying their men. I emphasize MEN because we want to avoid the man/child—silly, childish, unavailable men will waste your time every time.

Again, this goes back to not having a strategy or clear idea of what you want. So you use these apps and wing it. No wonder you're frustrated, don't think they work or that they are full of losers.

Because you can't spot the 'no effort' men or creeps that are going to take you right back to square one again, and you end up accepting crumbs from bums. It's like Groundhog Day.

5. Fantasy Thinking

You have a story in your mind of exactly how the entire dating experience should go.

I get it! We all love romance. We all grew up watching the same movies, but there isn't only one real-life approach. If you like things a certain way or have certain expectations, you will need to communicate that to the guy. These days there are many ways to get in touch—email, text, or calls. And honestly, guys don't know what you prefer until you tell them.

Also, it's best if you were open-minded. Just because a guy doesn't say and do all of the smoothest things out of the gate doesn't mean he's not a great guy. Sometimes, the most charming men are the real players and the ones you want to avoid. I always say the only way a man has gotten so good at what to say and how to say it is with lots of practice. And I don't mean that as a compliment.

Okay, now that we know some of the mistakes to avoid, it's time to dive into the good stuff—applying a strategy that freaking works. And I promise you my 'Swipe Like a Guy Method' will help you detach from the initial loathe or lust fest you usually have with these guys. Follow my lead here, and you're going to raise your standards, turn your profile into a magnet for high-quality men, and learn to weed out the creeps so that you can make room for your perfect guy to show up. And more importantly, so you stop getting exhausted with all of the duds you've been dealing with up until now.

Please note that different techniques might only apply to certain dating apps.
The complete 'Swipe Like a Guy Method' works best on Bumble. It's my preferred dating app because not only does it have a vast pool to choose from, I know great guys are using this app.

This method has been perfected while using this particular app. It's not to say it doesn't work on other apps. I'm merely telling you you'll get the best results if you apply them on Bumble.

So whether you're on Bumble, The League, Hinge, Luxy, or any of the apps, whatever you're into, whatever you're on, the strategies will work. I find that the men on Bumble seem to have more of a sense of immediacy in meeting you. And that's what this all comes down to, am I right?

It all comes down to creating a system and formula to pre-qualify these guys quickly and get on a date soon. Then, rinse and repeat. That's what you're going to learn from this book. And that way, if you're following a system doing that and you're swiping like a guy, which I'm going to talk about in a minute, then you're not going to get as burned out by these dating apps.

You're not. If you do it the way I'm going to tell you and use this formula and strategy I've created, it will help speed everything along, but you have to stick with it. It's about raising your standards.

One more thing I want to clarify about dating apps. I talk to women of all ages, and some will say, "I'm on the dating apps." So I ask, "Which dating app?" And they'll say, "Match.com."

Okay, let me be clear about dating apps. There are dating apps like Bumble, Hinge, The League, and others. Those are dating apps. That's where everybody is if you're in a bigger city. The apps are also more modern, so they attract more people making the pool of quality men larger. But if you're in a small town, then maybe Match.com is your only option. But I want you to know it's a dating website and considered old school. It's not a dating app, but it still might be best for you.

CHAPTER 2

THE HIGH-CALIBER MAN

(and you)

I didn't intend to work with billionaires and multi-millionaires. Initially, I started my company to help everybody. But I fell into it, this specific niche of working with these super handsome, successful eligible guys not because they couldn't meet beautiful women. Yes, they could, in fact, all the time. But they needed someone to look out for them—someone with integrity to screen and be a gatekeeper for their love lives. These men are powerful and have a lot to lose if they make the wrong choice when it comes to love. Hey, but don't we all?

When it comes to sharing their life with someone for the long term, the men I work with want it all. And this is how I know everything it takes to find and attract them, but more importantly, to you, how to get them to seal the deal.

A big part of what a high-caliber man wants in a woman is for her to have her life in order and it together in every way. And this is where many women get confused. So pay attention. Successful, handsome, eligible men might swipe on you, might date you, take you to nice dinners, flatter you with compliments, take you shopping and take you to bed, but none of that means anything beyond a surface-level connection. And many women think, "Hey, I attract great guys all the time." And to that, I say, "That's terrific, but how long did it last, and where are they now? And by the way, what made that guy so great, exactly?"

Because the women I know, like you, aren't looking for a surface-level connection. The goal is to find your partner for life and to build a meaningful, long-lasting relationship.

So, I hope that I can help you ramp up your efforts in every way, from raising your standards to reigniting your excitement for dating and the dating apps so that you can attract the exact type of man you want for the long term.

What I'm going to share with you here is what I've learned from working with these billionaires and multi-millionaires over the years, but I'm not just talking about wealth or money. Even though I am in the business of working with very successful men, when I refer to a guy as a high-quality man, I don't necessarily mean that he has to be super-rich. Not at all.

A high-caliber man or a great guy can be a guy who's not rich. Super-rich won't always mean he's a high-quality man just like being a total hunk doesn't mean that he's not a creep.

I know some of you ladies want an affluent lifestyle, and why not? And a super cute guy too, and why not? Perhaps you're looking for that one guy in your town who is a total catch. That's great. What I'm going to share with you here will cover all of that as well.

But it all starts with you and how you're showing up. So let me share one of my favorite stories of a young woman I met not long after I began my matchmaking business.

Tani had recently moved to Los Angeles, and we became fast friends. She was a go-getter. Every time I saw her, she was one of the most put-together women I knew. This lady was on a mission. She made up her mind and knew what she wanted. She didn't expect it to fall into her lap and didn't have any misconceptions about what she needed to do to get it either.

She had a great job at such a young age, owned a condo with her sister, and lived in Santa Monica. When we met, she had a clear picture of the type of man she wanted.

I was in awe of Tani. Here was a woman who was bringing her A-Game to every part of her life. I never saw Tani when she wasn't completely put together from head to toe. Her outfits fit her to a tee. Tani's hair, nails, and make-up were always done flawlessly. She always looked perfect. You had to respect the hustle.

She wasn't looking to be anyone's arm candy. She wanted to find her perfect guy, have a family, and be part of a power couple. And she was unstoppable.

The first thing that got my attention was, Tani was clear on the type of man she wanted. So much so that she knew what kind of woman he would be physically attracted to, and she was honest with herself about that. So, Tani had a personal trainer and worked extremely hard to be the type of person that the man she wanted would want.

Tani dated like it was her second job. Years ago, she used Match.com, went to events, and did anything and everything she needed to do. All while keeping a positive attitude. I'm telling you, she could not be deterred from her vision. Bad dates happened. She occasionally got rejected by guys she liked. She even found out a guy she had been dating for several months was cheating on her. But she never gave up or stopped bringing her A-Game. She kept at it. We eventually lost touch over the years but recently reconnected.

Guess what? Tani is now happily married to a handsome, successful guy (literally the man of her dreams) and has two beautiful baby boys. They have a beautiful home, and she is still the go-getter she was when we met so many years ago. This is a woman who got it all by bringing her A-Game and being unstoppable. And it was only possible because she had a clear vision of the life and man she wanted and was willing to do her part to ensure she got it.

The moral of the story is over the years, I have personally observed men and women who are unstoppable on their quest to find love, and they always end up getting it. As long as they have a clear vision and plan, they realize they need to be what their dream partner is looking for, and they pursue it relentlessly with an upbeat attitude. I always say, "Never lower your standards, be willing to work for it, and you'll get what you want."

As we set you up for success, remember to have a clear vision of your goals and the type of guy you want. But, when I say never lower your standards, what I mean is, never let someone treat you in a way that is less than you deserve. So when it comes to you saying, "He has to be tall" or "He has to be fit" or whatever it is, try to allow for some wiggle room. I see too many women remain single because they aren't showing up as the person an A-Game man wants. So remember that looks will fade at the end of the day, but the character of a person lasts forever.

Ready to turn up the heat? Let's optimize your profile....

CHAPTER 3

OPTIMIZING YOUR PROFILE

Attract the BEST

Okay, I know you're done with attracting those men who make you wish you weren't straight but don't give up yet. Yes, the dating apps are crowded. But I will say that is both the good part and bad part about them. You're showing up to a party filled with all types, and Mr. Right is among them. Somewhere, I promise. So how do you sift through the noise?

Your profile. This is why it's important to make sure your profile acts as a gatekeeper for you. This is the best way to start weeding out the duds while attracting the right men you want to meet.

So if you found yourself cringing in the first chapter about your profile, it's because you probably made many of the mistakes I mentioned. The majority do. It's all good. We are about to fix that. This is where my advice might freak you out. You need to take your deal breakers, what's most important to you, and the type of man you want, and you have to list that in your profile. Yep!

- *If you want a baby—say it (there are ways to say it without shouting it in desperation). For example, I love my life and career, but I am looking forward to starting a family in the next couple of years. If that turns guys off—GOOD—you saved yourself from wasting time.*

- *If you want an educated, goal-oriented man—say it. For example, I enjoy intellectual and thought-provoking conversations. I'm looking for a partner who is educated, successful, and who loves personal growth.*
- *If you want a man who is successful or who has money as you do—say it. For example, I am very successful in life, and I am looking for the same in my partner.*
- *If you want a man that's not hung up on the past and excited about the future—say it. For example, I'm looking ahead and excited about new adventures in life. If you have unresolved issues or hung up on the past, you'll be great for someone, just not me.*
- *If you want to get married (if that's your goal)—say it. For example, I'm looking for my next husband (joking). I want to see if you're paying attention. But seriously, try this instead—I am looking for someone to spend the rest of my life with, hopefully.*

Stop being afraid to say it.

If you're wondering why you aren't attracting the right men for you, this is why. Your profile needs to weed out the men who aren't a match for you. The players, time-wasters, and boys. Because first, you have to turn the wrong ones away to make room for the right ones to show up. Don't be afraid to turn anyone off. The ones that get turned off aren't the ones you want. Remember that. Be fearless.

I'm here to help you create a profile that will stand out among the crowd and make the men who are smart, attractive, and relationship-ready swipe right on you. First, I want to address one of the biggest questions I get asked, which is, "Should I put my real age?" I don't mind anybody fudging about their age, as long as it's not by more than two years.

There are many reasons why you don't want to stretch that lie beyond a couple of years. I know this is a touchy subject, but think about how you would feel if you were duped if he lied about his age. Well, ladies, he will feel the same way. Plus, no quality relationship starts with a lie.

We want to make sure your profile reflects that, okay! Because I think that's one of the biggest problems with these dating apps. It's become a popularity contest where people want to see how many swipes and matches they can get. So they set their profile up to get approval from the masses.

We don't want to do that, ladies. The more honest and specific you make your profile, the more you create a filter, which will curate better matches for you. We are only trying to target the men who are genuinely attracted and interested in who you are in every way.

There is no point in attracting a man who only wants a super-thin, very fit woman if you don't show up that way in person. There is no point in attracting a man who only likes your filtered photos. There is no point in attracting a man who swiped on you because your photos were from five years ago. There is no point in attracting a man who isn't looking for the same things you are in life.

Got it?

Okay, first, let's start with your photos. Three photos are all you need. But if you want to add more or can't decide, make sure it's a maximum of four photos. Anything more, and the men aren't looking at them, or they start to read into it. So please don't confuse them with a ton of pictures. If you do, they'll begin to think things like...

"Oh my God, she's really into herself."
"Is this even what she looks like now, or was that from 10 years ago?"
"I can't see her body. She must be hiding something,"
"Wow, she's a sex pot—she must be up for a good time,"
"Does she ever smile?" and
"Looks too high maintenance for me."

No Bueno. So you want to make sure your photos are current ones. We've all heard the horror stories of people showing up on dates only to find out the person looks nothing like their photos.

So, when you're picking your photos make sure it represents you as you are right now.

Here are the three photos you need of YOU and no one else. If you love a photo of yourself, but other people are in it, crop them out of it.

1. Clear straight-on headshot: No professional photos. Men want to see real. You can take one with your phone. But make sure it's with the best possible lighting. That way, it is the most flattering for you. And no filters, ladies, or at least NONE of those silly ones.
2. Body shot: Show them how you look. Big, little, or whatever size, it doesn't matter. Make sure they can see your body. If that's wearing jeans and a T-shirt or a tasteful, fitted dress, take this opportunity to show your style and what they can expect you to look like when you show up in person.

Things you want to avoid for your photos are:

- Bikini pics—the exception to a bikini photo is organic, which means you're on a boat, surfing, or playing beach volleyball. If you have photos like that, then yes, it makes sense to have a photo of you in a bikini. But if you are posing in a bikini with no pool or beach in sight, then it comes off as, "Look at me, I'm so hot." And the problem with that is his mind goes straight to the gutter if you know what I mean.
- Sunglasses—let them see your eyes.
- Looking too serious, not smiling—men want to see a happy smiling lady. That no-smile look is only suitable for Instagram.
- Hats—let them see your entire face.
- Too far away—we don't want to make them squint.
- Childish filters—you know the phony look or has butterflies on your face.
- No group shots with other women—men hate seeing these group shots. They don't know who you are. You may not realize you look like your friends, or even worse, your friends are better looking than you. You don't want to be in a picture with a group of women on the apps.
- No children—we don't want them assuming you have kids if you don't. Kids don't belong in your photos on a dating site.
- Overtly sexual photos—if you're complaining about d*ck pics or not meeting great guys, take a hard look at the type of photos you're posting.

True story, I've never received a d*ck pic in all my years on social media or dating apps.

Why?

I'm not posting racy photos that show it all. I'll post pictures where I look great wearing a classy, sexy dress. You can never go wrong with classy and sexy. Also, men will try to read into things that aren't there even if you don't have racy photos in your profile.

A woman that reached out to me couldn't figure out why she was getting crude and overtly sexual messages. I looked at her photos, and while she wasn't wearing anything racy, she did have her legs spread open in several photos. Even with jeans, when I looked at it as I do from a male perspective, I knew if a pervy dude wanted to see that as a sexual invitation, they would. Unfortunately, in her case, they did. It's not right; it's not fair, but if you get many inappropriate messages, take a closer look at what you might be unknowingly saying in your photos.

Figure out a way to show your body but in a tasteful, elegant way. You don't need to go overboard trying too hard, but you want to appear happy, sexy, classy, and cute. And they want to see what your body looks like in the photos. This is where you have to be honest so that there are no surprises. Some surprises are good, but not when you don't match the person they expected to see.

Okay, I've shared a lot about photos, now I want to make sure we cover your bio and profile details. We want to be direct here, ladies, and share what makes us fun, engaging, and unique without sharing our entire life story.

Now, if you want the type of men I work with—the extreme high achievers who have it all—keep in mind these men want smart, attractive, fit, and interesting women. I call this A-Game. Suppose you want an A-Game man. You have to be an A-Game woman. And believe me, looks are important, but that's not the only criteria.

So, never hold back on sharing your greatness. High-caliber men, the great ones, want to know things that average men with average lives don't care about learning. So always make sure to include in your profile your...

- Education
- Profession
- Travel experience
- Achievements
- Your passions

Remember, the men are looking to get a sense of who you are and what you bring to the table.

Average men, time wasters, or creeps don't care if you're smart. It might turn them off, which is FANTASTIC. That's the idea here.

The way to attract the best men, the men you want to meet, is to be as authentic and awesome as possible. This is where the magic is going to happen because A-Game attracts A-Game.

If your profile is ready to go, the pictures are set, you've stated what you want and how great you are, then all that is left right now is to start SWIPING! Oh, and make sure you double-check your age parameters and location settings.

Here's where it's about to take a speedy crazy turn, ladies, so hang on.

CHAPTER 4

SWIPE LIKE A GUY

Flip the Script on Them

What I'm about to share with you will freak you out because I'm going to get you to swipe like a guy.

It's going to scare you because women take the initial swiping too seriously. It's a fact. Ladies, we hope that these guys are at least looking at your pictures or reading your profile before they swipe on you, but most of the time, they're not. So the only way to know if a guy likes you, is to work the strategy I am about to give you.

A big mistake is that women take it too seriously at the beginning of the 'window shopping' phase on dating apps. You ladies are looking through all of their pictures, reading all the details, and you're giving it thought and time. Then you're only swiping if you like the guy. So when he matches with you, you get excited, which is usually followed by a letdown. Once this happens a few times, you are DONE with that dating app, and you delete it, only to reinstall it later. This pattern goes on over and over again.

Do you know what the guys do? I swear to you, this is what they do! They treat it as a game. So they glance at the app, your picture (maybe a second one), and they swipe. That's it—not looking or altogether paying attention. They figure it's only harmless fun. Once it is a mutual match, the guy will take a minute to look through all of your photos and skim your information.

Again, depending on the guy, they still aren't too invested, but once you match with him or signal that you're interested and he takes a closer look, that's when he realizes, "Oops, I'm not interested in her." Even though you send a message or respond to something he's written to you—poof he's gone. Why? Because he was never paying attention until he MATCHED with you or knew that he had your attention. That's when he went in and did a deep dive on your profile. In other words, this dude wasn't into you after all. He was swiping to see who liked him.

This is confusing and frustrating for you ladies, but I think the guys are on to something with their detached swiping. Let's face it, you rarely ever hear a man say that he hates dating apps. But you hear it from women all the time. And why? Because we take it too seriously and invest too much thought and energy into every swipe and every match. When during the first phase (i.e., window shopping)—the guys are watching TV or talking to their friends doing other things while they swipe away.

These apps are a game for men, and they are using them as a pastime. And I happen to know this as a fact. Now, I'm sure some men are taking it more seriously, but the majority are swiping on you ladies and not even looking. They're swiping to see who swipes on them. So when you match with them, it means nothing. It doesn't indicate that he likes you. Here's the deal, many times, the guys are trying to see who wants them.

This is where my strategy comes in. I recommend that you test to see which of these men on the dating apps genuinely likes you versus the jackasses who want to waste your time. If that is what you want, then listen closely to what I am about to tell you.

Here's what you're going to do:

SWIPE without any attachment to whom you are swiping on.

Swipe away! We're not thinking, and we don't care at this stage. Swipe, swipe, swipe, swipe like a banshee. Go to town, ladies. Let's see who will be the last man standing. Remember swiping and matching means nothing. We want to see who among these men are the ones who are truly interested in you.

You're going to go onto the apps and do this first part as a test. You don't have to do it forever. But you should stick with the overall formula for at least 30 days. However, this first part I want you to try a few times. And this is where no fear comes into play. Because I know you ladies, and I know it's going to scare the hell out of you, okay?

So, try it to see what happens, only as an experiment. Men are not afraid to swipe on any and every woman to see who likes them because they know that they can go in and unmatch with you, or they never follow up. Men don't care and have no guilt or fear about doing this, and neither should you.

Men are automatically born and raised to be fearless. We, as women, are raised to be careful and polite. For this experiment's purposes, I want to instill in you this no fear concept.

You're not going to look at them or study their profile. OK, I know you ladies, and I'll say, "Sure, look a tiny bit, but only barely—so that you aren't matching with the ones who look like they were just let loose from an asylum." Please try it. Trust me and try it. Let's test to see which guys are genuinely interested in you. How will you know? Well, on Bumble, a guy can extend the time, which is a way for him to demonstrate his real interest in wanting to connect with you. But more on that in a minute.

Please try it tonight, tomorrow, or whatever. Try it a few times. I know it scares you to do it, but who cares. It's a game at this point, and the guys do it the same way. We're flipping the script on them, ladies. It'll be interesting to see how many of these guys are willing to make an effort to show genuine interest in you. Is it 10, 20, or 30? And listen, don't sit around and obsess or freak out and think, "Oh my God, that guy's hideous. Oh, he likes me. I'm disgusted," or get upset if hardly anyone extends the time. This is why it's best not to invest too much time into whom you're swiping on. The matches don't matter. It's who cares enough to extend the time that matters here for this experiment.

And to be honest, the waiting part is something you should always do on Bumble. The experiment part is the swiping without really looking.

Now, if you're saying to yourself, "No way, this won't work. What if this? What if that?" Then hang on there lady, you're overthinking it. I'm trying to get you out of your head so that you're not overthinking. We're doing what the guys do.

Remember, right now; we're not even thinking at all.

Now you might say to me, "Gina, how am I going to know who likes me? If I have to write first, on Bumble? I'm not going to write to that guy. Are you kidding me, Gina? I'm not writing to that guy."

Calm yourself. Don't freak out yet. On Bumble (and this is why I like Bumble), if men are smart enough (and let's face it, you only want the smart ones, right?), they know there is a feature where they can extend the time for you to connect with them. I have heard you ladies say many men don't know about that feature blah blah blah. Come on, stop making excuses for these guys. The truth is if he matched with Kate Beckinsale, don't you think he would do anything and everything he could to figure out how to extend the time for her to write him back? Please don't kid yourself. This is where you find out fast who is and who's not interested.

This feature of extending the time lets men on Bumble do what I call—raise their hand. This allows you to know that they're interested.

I also have a system for Hinge and The League. But for this book, I want you to use Bumble as this feature to extend the time is excellent. The men can extend the time. Then you have 24 hours to write to them when you match with somebody.

When I started working with Melissa, I told her to try the swipe like a guy test. At first, she didn't make any changes to her photos or profile. She started swiping on about 30 guys and matched with about 20 of them. She was excited. But then, none of them extended the time. She was so upset and disappointed. She even said, "Gina, I like so and so, he seems perfect for me. Time is almost up—can't I write to him?" And I said, "NO!"

Then, I went through Melissa's photos and told her which ones to ditch and which ones to post. I also went through her profile and saw exactly why she wasn't attracting the really good guys who wanted to make an effort to extend the time. I fixed that too.

Then she went back to swiping blindly and working the strategy. This time she matched with about ten guys, and three extended the time. She was excited about two of the guys. And I am happy to report, she's dating one of them, and they are still going strong.

So, never write to them if they haven't made an effort beyond swiping, no matter what app you're using. Swiping, as you know now—takes no effort. Even if you think he's the most perfect guy in the world. If it was Brad Pitt, do not write to him. I can already hear what you're thinking., "Screw you, Gina! It's Brad FREAKING Pitt!! What the hell kind of advice are you giving me here? And Why?"

Here is why...

Chances are that good old Brad swiped and didn't even look at all of your photos or information. I'm telling you, ladies, I do this for a living. I talk to men all the time, so I know what they do. And I had my dating app, so I watched what they did on the back end. I would see what was happening. They would swipe swipe swipe on every lady. Even if it is Brad Pitt or Jason Momoa (if he were single), if he is the no effort man—you have to let him go.

I'm telling you right now, if you work the strategy on Bumble, which is you swipe and wait, only correspond with the guys who raised their hands. The ones who show you that they like you enough to let you know that they want to hear from you. This is a man who is genuinely interested in you.

Now you've pre-qualified these guys who are interested in you.

In the beginning, I'm going to prepare you. You may do pretty well right away once you optimize your profile but, not everybody does. And that's okay! Remember, you don't want everyone or anyone who isn't excited about you. You may freak out if only one guy extends the time and doesn't look like Brad Pitt or Jason Momoa.

Meanwhile, you matched with a Chris Hemsworth look alike, but he hasn't extended the time, and he's about to be gone for good. And right about now, you're saying to yourself, and to me, "Gina, I can't believe I can't write to him. Are you insane? I'm going to write to him anyway." Well, okay, then write to him, but know you're not working the strategy. Therefore if you end up wasting time and getting your hopes up for a guy who ends up being a no effort guy, you can't say I didn't warn you.

This filtering system is crucial. Don't you want to know if these guys are interested and not just swiping blindly on you? Of course, you do. This is how you're going to start pre-qualifying them.

And if you don't get the results you want, that tells you one of two things.
1. You need to target a different type of man.
2. You need to improve your photos or profile.

Good news! Finally, a great one extended the time. HOORAY!

Hang on a second, are you sure he's worth getting excited about so soon?

This is where we do what the guys do (remember flipping the script on them) before we message. It's time to give his profile a real look. That's right; you haven't bothered until now because it didn't matter. Now it's getting real, so let's take a look to see if we need to hit the brakes and unmatch with this guy and move on before investing in real-time.

CHAPTER 5

WEED OUT THE CREEPERS

What to Look for in His Profile

Now that you've done the pre-pre-qualifying by assessing who is blindly swiping versus the interested guys, we can take the strategy one step further. But as you go along in the process, you aren't always going to swipe on men blindly. You do that only a few times to round up as many specimens as possible to get a more accurate read on who among them is willing to step up (beyond the bozo's who've swiped). Which you know now—MEANS NOTHING.

Now that you set up your profile in a way that turns off the ones you don't want, and you're clear on the strategy of swipe without being invested, you'll start to use more tips I'm giving you here. This will help you evaluate and further pre-qualify these guys so that you can weed out the creepers.

Let's get down to business. First, I have a strong opinion about how to weed out these so-called creepers. And I know that's the favorite thing ladies want to know.

When I say creepers, it means a lot of different things. It certainly means the guys you don't want to meet. It means the guys who want to meet you, but they don't have anything going on for themselves. I like to refer to this guy as the no effort guy. So, out of the gate, I'm going to tell you how to spot these guys.

As we age, our social circles get smaller, and we aren't going out as much (or when we can't physically go out at all), yet still, our dream guy might only be a swipe away. And this is an invaluable resource that gives you access to as many men as possible. But the key is knowing which ones to go for, how to attract them, and which ones to avoid.

For example, someone who isn't showing up seriously on the dating app is not someone you want to waste a second of your time on. If the men put minimal to no effort into their profiles, this is an indicator of the effort he will put in if you date him. If he knows he's hot and thinks all he has to do is show up and post one or two pictures with no information—PASS.

And pay attention to the details because the information he puts down about himself is telling. A man who wants a real quality relationship will tell you all about what he does and what he's looking for in a woman.

- If a man won't put his occupation, that's a man not too happy or proud with what he does for a living.
- If a man says, "He isn't sure about the type of relationship he wants." PASS. You need a grown man who knows what he wants.
- If you see a man in his 50's say he wants kids—that usually is a code word for, "I want to date younger women," —PASS.

Many guys on these apps play games and waste your time because they aren't in the same rush women are, right? And I know women reading this are in different stages of their lives. So if you're a woman who wants to start a family, then you can't afford to waste time on these losers or creeps, and honestly, none of us do.

You want a man who looks and acts like he's all in, whether it's on the dating apps or even in person. So again, you want to look out for in the no effort, guys. The guy that doesn't give you much to work with, in a message, lack of information on his profile, or if he acts like it's one big joke. I mean, some of these things are obvious.

First, you have to raise your standards. Because I see too many of you women out there accepting what my friend Karen, who's married with an A-Game life, great husband, and kids, Karen would say, "I decided long ago never to accept crumbs. If a guy ever gave me crumbs, I would walk away."

Over the years, I have talked to many women who are often confused about whether they're in a relationship with a guy. A guy they've been sleeping with and dating. I hate to break it to you, but if you're confused about whether or not you're in a relationship with him, you probably aren't dating. And if you try to rationalize by saying that the guy you're supposed to be in a relationship with is so busy with other things in his life that he hasn't made time to see you in a week or two—chances are you're not in a relationship with that guy.

He isn't a high-quality guy and not worth your time, all right? You have to raise your standards and be willing to draw a line in the sand about what you will and will not tolerate.

And straight from the horse's mouth, here is a real-world example of a guy on a dating app wasting time. I was on a radio show on Valentine's Day. It was this guy's sports show, but he wanted to talk about dating apps. He said, "Yeah. So when I was on the dating apps, I don't know how you feel about this, Gina, but I had silly and ridiculous pictures."

And he said, "Then I decided to try something kind of out there. So on my profile, I wrote, looking to rob a bank. Who's with me?" Can you imagine the thoughts going through my head as he said this?

Now ladies, keep in mind this guy is one of those hot buff guys, so he thinks he can be funny and get away with it. So, I responded by trying my best not to say, "Geez, dude, what a jackass move." So instead, I said, "That's an angle. And I can appreciate the uniqueness. But my guess is that you weren't looking for anything serious, were you?"

And I called him out on it. And he said, "Well, I wasn't sure." He had to admit to it.

I mean, all of his pictures looked like jokes, and what he put was ridiculous. So if you are a serious woman looking for a serious guy, that is not the guy for you. But being such a cute guy, women will excuse the nonsense. Hoping he's better than his profile. That is not the case. And it's best if you take it at face value.

Also, you know, ladies, this is not what you want. You don't want a man who is unsure of what he wants—that is so unattractive. If he is unsure, that is a code word for, "Wants to date and have fun." That's it!

Setting a clear vision of what you want is the first step to any strategy, whether it's about dating, business, or life. You have to go in having a clear idea of the type of man you want, combined with what you're looking for and what you have to offer in return.

It's a two-way street. Make sure if you want a high-caliber one-of-a-kind man that you are showing up as a one-in-a-million kind of woman. If you are looking for an A-Game quality man, you must be an A-Game quality woman.

So ladies…

BEWARE OF THE MEN WHO WASTE YOUR TIME

I have another story to share with you about a woman named Lisa that I was helping. She was intelligent, capable with a fantastic career; she was a beautiful woman and kept herself in great shape. But she never made it stick with any of the guys she dated. It looked like she was bringing her A-Game, yet she never met the type of man who would commit to her for the long term.

I got to know her better as we started working together, and she believed she was picking all the right guys. She thought she was doing everything right. But when I started talking to her about the various guys she was swiping on or the ones she met at events, it turns out she had a specific criterion of her perfect guy. So she only paid attention to younger guys or guys right around her age. The problem with that is, in Los Angeles, a woman at 35 and a man at 35 are in two different time zones, which means they aren't on the same time clock. You might be in the same city, but not at the same place in terms of goals. Let me add—yes, there are exceptions, and you might even know of someone who is the exception. But that is not the norm.

I'm not here to burst anybody's bubble, but I am here to guide you in a direction so that you can make more intelligent choices. It boils down to you raising your standards. This woman needed to be more open-minded on finding an A-Game man who could meet her where she was at in life, rather than trying to find a guy who met her age criteria, hoping to convince him to move at a faster pace.

Ladies, you need clear boundaries for your goals and know when to turn these guys down who will waste your time. And it would help if you had a clear path to the men who aren't going to waste your time, who are there for the right reasons, and who want you. I'm here to steer you in the direction of men on the same page with the same goals in mind as you.

These guys around your age range, especially if you're in the late thirties, early forties, will date you. They'll also waste your time because they are not on the same time clock. But for you, dating is time-sensitive if you want to start a family. You don't have time to waste. I know this because I talk to these guys all the time. Guys around your age range, in their late thirties, early forties, want women in their early thirties for long-term committed relationships. Again, they'll date you, they'll swipe on you, but you'll find that they rarely put a ring on it. Don't kill the messenger. I don't want to see you waste your time.

Please find a guy that's ready. So if you're in your late thirties, early forties, beware of the younger guys. There are always exceptions, but I'm here to help you swipe on the men who are ready for a committed relationship.

I know it's flattering when younger guys pay attention to you. If you want fun and you're not looking for commitment, go for it. But if you are looking for a long-term relationship, younger guys won't go the distance. Sure they might be attracted to you because you're pretty, sexy, or there's magic in the air. The truth is they are likely attracted to you because you have more than they do, and they find that exciting. Similar to a younger woman who wants to date an older man. Why would she date him over a young stud? Because he has access to a nicer life, things, or maybe he can help her somehow.

So back to Lisa, she was connecting with all these younger guys. Finally, we started working together, and of course, I had her open up the age criteria to be more realistic. We started meeting through Zoom, and together we did swipe sessions. She would hold up her phone, and I would guide her on whom she needed to be choosing. I steered her in the direction of men that I felt were more appropriate for her, and it opened her eyes. She met a great guy. He was ready, she was ready, and last I talked to her, things were progressing nicely. But helping her was a combination of things. I came up with a strategy for her, which was crucial to her success. The unique approach I included—how to see him, in plain sight. Most of the time, we overlook the great guys who are right in front of us. She had specific things she was interested in, and she wanted a man who aligned with them. I helped her get clear on this to start targeting the right guys, and I helped her get out of her own way.

Now taking this offline. There are many missed opportunities every day. If you're at Starbucks, finding high-quality men is as easy as being off your phone, looking up, making eye contact, and smiling at these guys. I look around, and I see women who look cute, but they are not smiling or friendly—not looking at anyone around them. They have their faces firmly planted on their phone screen. And you know, I even had other matchmakers talk to me about this too.

They say, "Single women need to get off their phones if they're in a public place like a Starbucks, a grocery store, or at a restaurant waiting for somebody."

Why?

Because it's a prime opportunity to put the phone away and look up, you're around people ladies, the friendlier and happier you appear, the more people you will attract. Also, chat with people—random strangers. The more you do this, the more people you're going to meet.

The problem is we are so attached to our phones or plain fearful of chatting with strangers that we've forgotten the art of harmless flirting, so we miss opportunities right in front of us. You have to stop all that. I go more in-depth into various A-Game strategies to meet the best men in person in my A-Game video course.

Just remember, it's flattering to get the attention of younger guys, but make sure that they're the right guys for you and that they're not going to waste your time, and that they are on the same page as you.

I bet right about now you are scared sh*less to get started with this, or you are raring to go to the next step—so I'm about to push you into the deep end. Let's say you have a great guy on the hook now. This process will go even faster. If you message correctly, it should be fun and painless so let's get into that now!

CHAPTER 6

HOW-TO MESSAGE

Think of it as a Tennis Match

One of the questions I get asked the most is, "How do I start the conversation? Should I, or should he?"

Well, if we're talking about Bumble, once he extends the time, it's up to you to start the actual conversation. If you're using another dating app, and he can write first, then he should write first. This is equivalent to extending the time (meaning to show effort) as he did on Bumble.

So if you're on another dating app, let him message you first, then game on. Hopefully, he opens with a question to which you answer and ask him a question in return.

Now on Bumble, you're writing first, but the good news here is, there's an easy way to get the tennis match going; that is, to be a success, it has to go back and forth. Because it takes two to play a tennis game, just like it takes two to keep a conversation going, got it. So, you want to say, "Hi," and ask a question. But never just, "Hi." That puts it all on him, which I don't mind, but to be fair, let's help him out a bit. I always recommend men and women reference something that you saw in their photos or what they put in their profile. You want to start with a light, playful conversation, so it opens the door for these men to walk through. From there, we see if the guy is willing and able to make interesting conversations.

The goal here is to cut to chase quickly so that you're not wasting your energy on the 'no effort' men. Because, ladies, the 'no effort' men are everywhere. The basics of what you're looking for in this messaging phase is to see if he asks questions about you, as you should be asking questions about him. If the guy only talks about himself, it's not good; if he doesn't have a lot to say, not good; or if you are the one keeping this conversation alive, not good. Please pay attention to these things and don't ignore them. This way, you're not investing time and getting frustrated when things don't work out down the line.

We want the men who are excited to learn about you and who are going to put in effort from the start, right?

So, let's walk through a scenario on how you want these conversations to go. Starting with you saying hi, and asking a question.

"Hi John, looks like you love golf? I've played a few times, or I've always wanted to go."

Now you see how this gives John something to work with so that he can respond. I believe in always giving them a little starter.

Now, if he comes back with "Hi," and nothing else, it's not a good sign, or if he comments on golf as it relates to him, I can already tell you he's not trying that hard to win you over. That's a bad sign, ladies!

But if you think he's especially cute or other things about him excite you, you can throw him a bone. Men can be nervous too. Plus, I often tell women that men are confused about what to do these days. They don't know if you want to be texted or called. They don't know what to say sometimes, and that's okay because you don't want the smoothest guy in the room either.

Right?

You know the super attractive, smooth-talking guys that are laying on the moves. The thing is, all the women are attracted to this guy. And he knows it! Remember that!

So we want to give the guy a little room to step up his game. So, if he doesn't ask a question back or say much more than some bland answer, I want you to ask him another question. But this is his last chance.

Hopefully, he responds with the answer to that question. And asks you a question back. If he doesn't, sorry, but it's time to walk away and move on. Unmatch. Pull the plug, don't look back. I know it might come off as harsh or too quick to judge, but I promise you, you'll end up resuscitating this thing over and over. I tell women all the time this is why you're exhausted. You expect these 'no effort' men to change. They aren't changing. Plus, why the heck would you want to try and change them? There are so many other fish in the pond, I say throw him back and reel in another.

So, ladies, do not try to keep it going because this is how you end up getting involved with these guys that put in no effort. I don't care if he looks cute. I don't care if he sounds cute. I don't care. And nor should you.

We want the guy to make an effort for you. That's what we're after here. That's the purpose of the strategy and the filter.

Got it?

Great! Let's pretend he's answered your question and asked you a question back. Now you're off to the races, and you follow up with a question. There's a little back and forth. It should never be all one way. You don't want to be a taker. You don't want him to be a taker. It should be a friendly little tennis match.

After a few messages back and forth, you need to move it off the app to a call. Honestly, I don't let this thing drag on at all–three to four messages at most. So we're going to nip it in the bud and move it along to a call. I'm not a fan of you asking him for his number. But there is another way to take the lead and move it along. If he seems like he wants to keep chatting more on the app, it's time to let him know; you'd prefer to get on a call by simply saying: I'm not on this app that much and not really into messaging but you can give me a call. Then wait and let him take your cue and ask for your number. This is just one approach, there are many.

You might have a few tennis matches happening with different men. So better to move them off of messaging and on to a call to determine the next steps. In other words, don't keep a lot of little fires burning.

Let's recap with this possible scenario:

You: "Hi John, I see you like Golf. Where do you play?" or "Hi John, where in New York do you live?" (that is as simple as it gets)
John: "Hi, Jessica, I try to golf as often as I can. Usually at blah blah golf course. Have you ever played?"
You: "Twice. It was fun. But, I'm more of a tennis gal." See what I did there? I am bringing it back to you and what you like to do to see if he will step up and ask more about you.
John: "Tennis. I love tennis too. Have you played recently?"
Ok—so at this point, you guys are off to a great start—you both like outdoor sports—that's great. And he is engaging with you and trying to get to know you better.

At this point, if you like him, your next message should go like this:

You: "Not in a while, I'm overdue (insert tennis emoji, it's cute and playful). Here's my number 310-888-9977. Feel free to give me a call." He'll be saying to himself, "Thank God I got her number, finally a lady not into games."

Remember, move it along as quickly as you see there is a mutual interest. The worst thing you can do is let this messaging drag on too long.

And I know what you're probably thinking, "Wow, that was quick. I'm not sure I'm ready to jump on a call yet," "Gina, I hate taking calls. What do I even say?" or "I don't want to look so desperate." If he likes you, he likes you. If he's looking for a relationship and he likes you, he'll want that number and will want to call you.

I understand many of you are more comfortable with texts over calls. It makes sense. We are so used to sending texts, but I promise the quicker you get on a call, the more you'll learn about this guy. And you can further weed guys out. If you're remotely exhausted with them, it's because you drag this nonsense on too long. My strategy is rapid-fire qualifying so that you reduce the frustration and overwhelm of wasting your time on creeps.

Now let's talk more about next steps.

CHAPTER 7

STOP WASTING TIME

Get Them on a Call or Video Date

As I've mentioned, women tell me all the time that they don't want to talk on the phone or do a video date. I get it! But here's the thing, do you want to get your hopes up before your date and make the time to get ready only to arrive to discover you hate his voice or something about him that you could have easily found out on a call or even better a video date? Once you get on the call, you'll get a feel for him. You'll hear his voice. And you get other important questions answered.

If you don't get on a call and skip right to an in-person date, you run the risk of ending up right where you were before. Angry and exhausted that you wasted time and frustrated with the dating apps. Yes, I know the drill. And then you'll try to blame me. I know what you're going to say, "Gina's formula doesn't work." But here's the thing—it only works if you do ALL of it. And that means you must go from a few messages on the dating app to a call.

Why do you need to take this step? Because a considerable part of this new plan I'm giving you is all about being smart and properly pre-qualifying these guys easily and quickly, so you don't hit burnout for the millionth time.

The call doesn't have to drag on too long. It should be 30 minutes max. No matter how good it's going. Once you hit the thirty-minute mark, you say, "Oh, I didn't realize the time, I've got to call my mom, my friend, I have to take the dogs out or drop off a package," whatever. Shortly, I'll tell you what to expect and how to proceed when you wrap up the call.

Ok—now you're clear not to miss this step, and hopefully, you understand it shouldn't be a long, drawn-out call.

Now let's dive into what is so important about a call. Well, it's easy to present yourself one way in a profile, and for some, it's easy to be fun and flirty in a few messages. More often than not, despite what the guys have written in their profile, you can uncover more about who they are, what they do, what they're really into, as well as if this is the right fit by asking a few key questions that are always better asked when you can hear their voice and vice versa.

For example, you can ask questions like:

1. Where do you live, and why? Do you live alone? Do you own a house? How long have you lived there? You want to get specific about where they live and who lives with them. For example, "John, what part of Burbank do you live? Usually, this will prompt him to tell you the 'why' behind where he lives. Then you can say, "Have you lived there long?" This will get him to open up about whether he rents or owns and who lives with him.

You'd be surprised to find out some men say they live in a ritzy or affluent area, but then you find out it's a guest house, condo, apartment, or they have a roommate. While none of those things might be deal breakers for you, trust me, other things will be revealed once his living situation is discussed. He might end up telling you he is not yet divorced or going through a transition in his life.

2. Is their goal marriage? Are they divorced or separated?

If you haven't found that out yet, there is nothing wrong with asking this question on the phone. Yet, so many women are afraid to ask. A call is the best and easiest way to find these things out. Face-to-face is where it can get awkward. Like the question above, his answer will lead the conversation to reveal other things.

For example, you can say, "How long have you been divorced?" This question is SUPER important to ask because many men act like they are divorced when in fact they aren't quite 'free and clear.' And if you don't ask, most won't volunteer it, at least not right away.

3. Does his life seem stable, is he rooted with a promising career (despite what he included in his profile), home life, friends, and family?

There is nothing wrong with inquiring about what he does for a living and even asking if he enjoys it.

4. If you're an animal person, it's best to know if they are.

Ha! I threw this one in for me. Too many men act like they love pets, but many think having a pet is as easy as simply having a doggie door. It's one thing to include it in a profile, but if it's a significant part of your life, this is where there needs to be more of a deep dive into how your lifestyles match.

5. If you're happy and love to go out to do fun things, he might have put that on his profile, but during the call, you should ask when was the last time he did X, Y, or Z.

These questions aren't the actual questions you have to ask, but use them as guidelines. It's best to ask him questions that are important and relevant as it pertains to you. You know, it's just like learning if he has kids or exes. You want to get a clear picture of his lifestyle.

A common mistake here is, even though we hear deal-breakers or things that aren't an ideal match for our lifestyle, we ignore it and think that that person or their situation will change. This is why so many relationships end. People ignore things they don't like, hoping that the other person will change or love them so much that they will become different. Wrong, ladies! This is what I call settling.

I'm trying to help a young woman right now who is down the rabbit hole in love with a guy who makes her constantly frustrated, upset, and there is non-stop bickering between the two of them. And she says, "Gina, I told him he needs to do this, he needs to do that, I wish he would stop blah blah blah." In other words, she wants him to be a different person than the person she fell in love with—I think we all know how that story will end. This is why I say, "Better to go in, never hoping Mr. Right will change because all that means is that he is not Mr. Right for you."

Only date someone if you are completely okay with who they are right now. And ask yourself—if nothing changes about them will you be OK with that in a year, two years, or forever?

Time to sort out those deal-breakers on a call. This is the beauty of dating apps. If used correctly, you can avoid so much time by asking key questions upfront. Now, this is important to keep in mind. You don't want it to seem like an interrogation. Always remember the tennis match scenario. Ask and answer a question, and make it an intelligent conversation between two adults trying to get to know one another without complete fluff. I like to laugh and am genuinely interested in learning about people. And because of it, I can get away with saying almost anything to anyone, as long as it sounds light-hearted and not coming from a place of judgment.

Any man that gets offended or weirded out by your questions is a guy who has something to hide or isn't looking for a serious relationship. So never be afraid to ask a question if that question is important to you.

Again, sprinkle in a bit of laughter and fun. Men often say women are too serious, guarded, and not playful enough. I understand that; imagine if you fired off these questions to him without humor or lightheartedness. It would come off as quite intense.

Think of it as a dance—salsa. Some moves are intense, sensual, playful, and fun. The conversation should go the same way.

Now I want to show you another dance move that I suggest. If the call goes well, as the call ends, hopefully, you guys have talked about going on an actual date. If so, fantastic, but may I first suggest a Zoom date? Again, this is a great step that can save you so much time.

So let's say the call goes well, but it's 30 minutes, and you say, you've got run. Now what? He didn't mention a date; in fact, he said, "Ok, I'll call you again." DO NOT let that happen. Arrrghhh, you don't need a new text buddy or phone call friend. Nope. Never get off that call leaving it in limbo.

Here are a few possible scenarios and how to deal with them:

Scenario #1: f you like him, and he says he'd like to call you again or asks when you guys can chat again. I want you to say, "Well, if you're up for it, I thought it might be fun to meet on a Zoom call next." See what he says. If he says sure, tell him when you're available, and set it up.

Scenario #2: If you like him, but he makes no mention of going out or talking again. This is likely an indication that he's not interested. And that's ok. You're pre-qualifying him, and he's pre-qualifying you. But unless he suggests something (a call or date), you say nothing more than it was nice talking to you and say goodbye. If he then calls or texts—refer to my advice above—and reply and say, "I thought it might be fun to get on a Zoom call." And set it up!

Scenario #3: If you like him, it went well, and he asks you out. My advice is to put him in the final pre-qualifying step still and get on a Zoom call. Now I know you ladies have a tendency to want to go for it, and ultimately it's up to you. But, if the goal here (and it is) is to create a system for you to connect with better men and pre-qualify them quickly, so you're only going out with the best—then you should follow all of the steps.

Scenario #4: If you don't like him, and he suggests getting together or talking again, always be polite and say, "You seem nice, and I appreciate your time, but I don't think we are a match." If you don't feel comfortable saying it on the call, you can say it in a text afterward. But it would be best if you came clean and never leave anyone hanging—that's bad form.

Now, let's talk briefly about Zoom. He can send you a link, or you can send him one. Ensure your lighting and angles are flattering, and be aware of what's in the background behind you. Practice with a friend ahead of time if you need to, and make this your go-to location for your Zoom dates. And make sure you put effort into your appearance.

Now you'll see if he looks like his photos, he has a fun personality, and even what his place looks nice or not. This will give you a fast track to it being a go or a no without ever having to leave your house.

When you end the Zoom date, if you like him, try to make sure there is an in-person date set up. Never leave it in limbo. Don't let him revert back to another Zoom, call, or text.

. He is a man who is ready and excited to meet you, or he's not. If he's not, it's bye-bye and on to the next!

Deanna was excited that she connected with a guy on Bumble. She followed my formula but ended up skipping the call and going straight to a Zoom date. She thought she was doing even more of a fast track to pre-qualifying the guy.

Initially, the Zoom date went well. Deanna liked him and thought he was cute, but as the Zoom call went on, he mentioned that he was doing it from a shared workspace.

Why, you might ask? Well, it turns out he was a 50-year-old man living with his elderly parents. And it wasn't because they needed his help. He went on to say that his life was in transition. When he moved back to California from Chicago, he had moved in with his parents temporarily. He moved back to California because he'd pursued a relationship in Chicago that had now ended. He said he only planned to live there briefly, but then COVID-19 hit, and he ended up staying longer.

So when did he move in with his parents? October of 2019, and hasn't left yet. That led us to talk about his career, which turns out was also in flux. He made it seem like he had a great career and a prestigious college degree on his profile, but for whatever reason, this guy had recently decided to start a T-shirt printing business.

After she told me this story, she said, "I wish I had a call with him first so that I hadn't wasted time getting ready, setting up my lighting, and getting on my computer. But I'm so glad I didn't go ahead and meet him in person, which is what I would have done in the past."

Ladies, keep in mind, there is nothing wrong with what that guy had going on in his life. But it wasn't what Deanna was looking for in a guy. She was an established woman with a career and house and wanted the same. She learned long ago never to date anyone whose life is in transition. So this guy wasn't the right fit for her and what she wanted. Interestingly enough, his profile drew her in because he listed he had a graduate degree and is an entrepreneur. Even in the messaging phase, he seemed cool and interesting. It was because she did the Zoom first (but many of these things she could also have found out on a call) that she got a clearer picture of his current lifestyle.

Now hang on before you say to yourself, "See another guy who looked good on paper but was like all of the others," or "Same sh*t different day. See Gina, no great guys on the dating apps."

You have to remember that dating apps are a crucial resource for you to use because it is popular with everyone. You might draw in guys that aren't ideal, but the point of this new system is to weed them out quickly while also attracting the guys you want. Hang with it, move quickly and move on when necessary. I'm not saying you are no longer going to get an occasional dud. I am saying that you'll be able to recognize them and throw them back in the pond much faster than before. This will save you so much time and energy. And spare you the usual frustration.

Also, stick to the plan and follow the formula no matter how excited you get. Oh, and on that note, ladies, you get too excited too soon. Wait until this person is real. Meaning, you followed the steps, you met in person, had a couple of dates, and it's gone well. That is when you get excited. Any sooner, and you are setting yourself up for a roller coaster of emotions on these dating apps. The quick highs and the even faster lows. And if you get on that roller coaster, it will bring you right back to dating burnout.

CHAPTER 8

ACING THE FIRST DATE

Like the Goddess You Are

Okay, by now, you're crushing it, and the in-person dates are starting to happen. I've seen dates go right. I've seen dates go wrong. I've seen women blow it. I've seen guys blow it. So hopefully, after reading this, you're a bit wiser.

Because if you like him, it's vital that you ace the first date so that he wants a second, third, and so on. But a critical strategy here is bringing your A-Game to these dates because that is what high-quality men are looking for in a woman.

Here are the dos and don'ts of dating:

1. BE ON TIME! Ladies, none of this five minutes late is okay, or my friend said ten minutes late is OK. It's not okay to be late. So make it a point that you're never late—early is even better than late. I learned this from my successful clients. They hate it when a woman shows up late, and these super busy, high-achieving men are always on time, to the minute. So, train yourself to get in the habit of being someone who respects other people's time and who takes pride in never being late.

2. I think most women know this, but I'm going to say it anyway because sometimes it needs saying. Put effort into your appearance. I know you might be tired of dating.

Tired of showing up and making an effort only to discover you don't like the guy. I get it! You're exhausted. So you're likely saying to yourself, "Another date, I probably won't like this guy." What do you do that one time, you don't put any effort into what you wear, or you decided not to do your hair. I know women that showed up on dates with their hair in a ponytail or unwashed. I had a client tell me once, "Gina, she didn't look like she did anything with her hair." And when I asked her about it, she laughed and said, "Oh yeah, I was rushed, so I didn't bother to fix it." She liked him, but he wasn't impressed, especially when he planned a beautiful romantic dinner.

Honestly, why bother showing up at all? No, ladies, if you are showing up, you are always dressed to impress. Remember A-Game ladies—A-Game.

I've heard this story from many women who said they made the mistake of showing up without putting any effort in, and then they ended up liking the guy. And they wished they had dressed better. They wished they'd spent a little more time on their appearance. And we all know, that's how life works, am I right?

The one time, you let your guard down. Show up when you know you don't look that hot —that's when you end up liking the guy (and then he might not be into you), or you end up running into an ex. I know you want me to say that he will like you anyway if you show up and don't look that hot, but the truth is it might not happen. So why take the risk?

So show up looking your best whether you end up liking him or not. Never phone it in. Put the effort in, ladies, if you're going to go to the trouble of showing up for a date. Especially if he's taking you on a date that he has planned and is paying for, then do both of you a favor and put effort into looking your best.

So you might be wondering now, "Okay, Gina, I get it. So what should I wear?"

You can't go wrong with classy and sexy. Of course, it also depends on where you're going, and you never want to show up in big clothes so that the guy can't see your body. I mean, come on. Layers! Uggghhhh, the worst.

That's another thing. When women fill out profiles for me and meet me in person (my job is to meet everybody in person), there's nothing more frustrating when they show up wearing layers of clothes or some flowy dress or never take their coat off.

I am there to assess it all. Yes, I want to see their personality. But beyond that, a big part of my job with meeting women in person is to check them out, head to toe. That is part of the matchmaking job, and I am there on behalf of my client. I need to see these women's front, back, side, face, and personality. I need to see it all—the total package.

That's how guys feel when they go out with you. So if you show up and you're wearing layers of clothing that you never un-layer and you're wrapped up like you're going to Alaska or a Lilith Fair concert (an old 90's reference), then the guys get bummed out. And more than that, what he's thinking is that you have something to hide.

Make sure that you dress to impress on a first date, and it fits the occasion. Classy and sexy, ladies. You can never go wrong when you look your best. So, if it's dinner, wear something that fits well and something that makes you feel feminine and flirty. Even if you insist on wearing pants and a top—make sure it still makes you feel sexy and flirty.

What if it's a daytime lunch? Jeans and a nice top with a cute jacket to polish the look works too. But make sure it hints at being a bit fun, sexy, and feminine.

Extra tip:

Suppose you find yourself dating during COVID-19 or any situation where you have to sit outside or where it's chilly. If you wear a coat, pick an outfit that allows him to see your body under the coat. Then, my trick is—at some point, even if you have to pretend you are warm enough (even for a minute), take off the coat. Maybe it's to walk to the bathroom, and you carry your coat with you.

Then you can always say, "Oh wow, it's colder than I thought," and put your coat right back on again. Works every time! Otherwise, he is going to sit there all night, preoccupied thinking, "What does her body look like?" Trust me on this. Even if you think to yourself, "Well, he's seen me in photos." Sure he has but in person is what matters.

Okay, switching gears here: No bragging about your ex. Oh, you dated this guy, and you dated this guy, and your ex was great. When it comes to recalling an ex's greatness (then why is he an ex?), people go to extremes here. And it seems like they're zero to ten. Either you're bragging about somebody, or you're telling this complete stranger how insane your ex is, am I right?

You never want to share how crazy your ex-boyfriend is or, even worse, how he stalked you and how you had to get a restraining order. So don't do either of those things. You don't want to brag. You don't want to intimidate somebody. And you don't want to make this guy think you got mixed up with a total psycho. This is the baggage you must keep to yourself. Don't unload any of those heavy things on a first date.

Oh, if you read my first book, Stop Being a B*tch and Get a Boyfriend, you know (among the many other personality types I talked about) to avoid showing up as the 'all-business lady.' Many ladies who are very career or work-focused get into big trouble about this on first dates. We slip into being the all-business-talk woman.

If you're going out with a guy who knows your industry or has connections to a career you, don't make it all about him giving you advice. I've known many women who are guilty of doing this type of thing. So keep in mind there's a balance of being inquisitive about somebody's job and what they do and having that good tennis match conversation where it's question and answer, question and answer. And that's how it should go. And sure, men make tons of mistakes, but in this book, I'm here to help you.

So keep it light and fun. But if you ever get so caught up in the moment with how smart he seems to be about things you need advice on, and all of a sudden, you want tax advice, and you say, "Who does your accounting?" You know you've taken it too far. Ten years ago, I caught myself on a date asking a guy who did his accounting. And I'll always remember the look on his face. Like what? He was adorable, I liked him, and at that moment, I blew it. I mean, it wasn't just that. It was at the beginning of starting my matchmaking business, and business was ALL I wanted to talk about.

It's easy to get excited about someone's knowledge and success, but business talk is not sexy. You always want to keep the first date (let me repeat it) light, fun, flirty and sexy. My guys tell me all the time that they want a woman to show up and be smart, yes, sexy, yes, but even more than any of that, they want a woman to be open and playful.

Vulnerable is the word they use. When women hear the word 'vulnerable,' they think it means the men want them to be weak. That's not it at all. When they say vulnerable, what they mean is women who are not guarded and hard.

The thing is, ladies, the older women get, the more guarded, opinionated, and serious we become. So you have to shake it off and lighten up.

Here's a quick recap for my skimmers (and I added in a few more):

BE ON TIME

LOOK YOUR BEST (SEXY, CLASSY, PLAYFUL)

BE FUN, INTERESTING, AND LIGHT

ALWAYS BE A LADY: KEEP IT CLASSY

NEVER DRINK TOO MUCH

NO BRAGGING

NO LOOKING AT YOUR PHONE

BE PRESENT IN THE MOMENT—ALWAYS

Doing these things will almost always get you a second date. Now whether you want another date with him or not, that will be up to you. But at least you brought your A-Game. And the more you fine-tune your A-Game in every way, the more you'll be ready when that perfect A-Game guy shows up. Don't worry. If you are confused about why I keep mentioning the A-Game, I'll explain that in the next chapter. In the meantime, let me share a story with you of a date gone wrong, VERY wrong.

And as a matchmaker and a woman, it was my worst nightmare. Keep in mind this story is about a beautiful grown woman with a great career. She wasn't some silly kid. I think sometimes attractive women who have great careers believe the rules don't apply to them. But the rules always apply to everyone. The rules apply even more so when you're going out with a high-quality A-Game man.

My client was very excited to meet this woman. I raved about her and was impressed with her when we met. So, based on my recommendation, he took his private plane to LA so that he could take her out to dinner. I made the reservation at one of the best restaurants in town. We had a car pick her up, so she didn't have to drive, and he met her there.

When she walked in, he thought, "Wow. What a knockout." She gave him a sweet hello and hug, then said, "Let's get drinks." She wanted to do tequila shots, so they had a couple of shots before they went to the table for dinner. At dinner, she turns into a party girl, ordering drink after drink. When dinner was done, my client was ready to get rid of her as fast as he could. As they were leaving the restaurant, she said, "Where are we going now?"

He informed her that he was going back to his hotel to meet his pilots for a nightcap. Without being invited, she said, "I'll join you!" She proceeded to follow him like a drunk puppy. And unfortunately, it didn't end there.

Once they were back at the hotel in the lobby bar, she didn't stop drinking. And while I think she thought she was funny, she was saying some pretty unrepeatable sexual things to one of his pilots.

At this point, these guys were so desperate to get rid of her that my client said, "Hey, we're going down the street to the cigar bar" (thinking a woman probably would have no interest in that). He was wrong. She insisted on going with them. And yep, you guessed it; she kept drinking. Now my client was also drinking—he's no saint. He is a classy guy, but a man is a man. It's getting late, and right about now, she's feeling sexy, hot, and horny, so she made no bones about showing it right in front of everyone at the cigar bar.

After kissing my client nonstop, it was very, very late by this time, and the cigar bar was closing. She jumps in the car with my client and his pilots as they head back to their hotel. Once back at the hotel, he says he will call her a car to take her home. She won't go. So he goes to the front desk and gets her a room. It turns out she wouldn't stay in her room, which was paid for and waiting for her. She insisted on following him to his room.

The rest, my friends, is history.

I met him for breakfast the next morning, and he told me this story. And all of the gory details. He said, "Gina, I didn't bring my plane here to meet a girl that I can meet anywhere in a nightclub." He was shocked, and I was mortified. Meanwhile, she thought the date went well, which dumbfounded me even more. She sent me a text saying, "Gina, we had such a good time last night. I was a little naughty, but we had fun! I'm excited to see him again."

Of course, there was no second date. I don't care who you are, how pretty you are, how smart you think you are; the rules always apply.

Ok, so this gal did not bring her A-Game, and that was obvious, but for those unfamiliar with the A-Game behavior and mindset, hang on. I'm laying it all out for you in the next chapter.

CHAPTER 9

THE A-GAME

You Have To Bring It Ladies

So you've heard me mention throughout this book about bringing your A-Game, A-Game men, and how to get an A-Game man—you need to bring your A-Game.

Now I want to share with you more about this A-Game concept. For me, it was life-changing.

These high-achieving men I work with for matchmaking have used this in their business, but you can use this strategy for any aspect of your life. And more than that, I have taken what I have seen them do in business, what I have seen them do in dating, and I translated it in a way so you can use it to your advantage.

The best part of what I teach in the A-Game course is that you can use these game-changing secrets for everything you do, and it's something that you can use at any age or any stage of your life.

It's about transforming your life from getting ordinary results to extraordinary results.

You can bring your A-Game to every aspect of your life. If something in your life isn't flourishing, then you'll be able to check-in with yourself and do an internal assessment and say, "Am I bringing my A-Game?"

For starters, it means being willing to put extraordinary effort into every detail of your life. And it's what most people aren't willing to do. It starts with taking responsibility for yourself in every way.

I first learned what it meant from my billionaire clients. You can only achieve greatness or a certain level of success if you bring your A-Game in every way.

I have watched what A-Game men like, what they do, what they don't do, where they go, don't go, what kind of women hold their attention, versus the ones they only take out a few times.

Let me stress, A-Game behavior is not limited to being a billionaire or multi-millionaire. And you don't have to want to be super rich or even want a super-rich guy. But if you want a great guy and a great life, then there are still fundamental details that you must do to achieve an A-Game life.

I applied it to my business, and it has taken me to the top of the matchmaking industry. Tani applied it to her love life, and as you know, she got the dream husband and life she always wanted. And Audri brought it to her efforts on the dating app and not only met many A-Game men but ended up getting married for the first time well into her 60's!

So if something in your life isn't flourishing, then you'll be able to ask yourself and do these internal check-ins and say, "Am I bringing my A-Game?"

As I mentioned above, the first time I heard about the A-Game was from one of my billionaire clients. And it changed my entire life because once he introduced me to these A-Game strategies, I used them to achieve everything I wanted. These are strategies that all these billionaires and multi-millionaires are using as well as every famous athlete, celebrity, and anyone you know who has achieved their dreams. What's their secret? They bring their A-Game.

Now, I wasn't born into the A-Game. I don't know if you were, but I was nowhere near bringing my A-Game. I didn't know what it was when I got introduced to it over ten years ago, but I used the A-Game strategies to transform my life. I still use some of them every day, and you can too.

I created a course—a video series that lays out how you can bring your A-Game to dating because I know many of you are so frustrated with dating these guys that are average and boring. These guys live an average existence, but just existing isn't living life with your foot on the gas. Life should be lived at full speed.

It's not about wanting rich men; it's about wanting a quality guy who's really putting effort into everything he does, which means you've got to start putting effort into everything you do to attract those A-Game, high-quality men.

I know so many women, who talk about the kind of guys they want, and they may even cross paths with these men. Still, if they're not dressing and acting the part, or if they're not bringing their A-Game, in every way and are prepared when they do happen upon this guy, then the opportunity is missed. And it might not come along again. It's competitive for anything worth having in this world. There is a barrier to entry. If there weren't a barrier to entry, then everybody would have everything they ever wanted in life quickly and effortlessly. The truth is, only a certain number of people achieve massive success, but this is the next level of effort most people aren't willing to put in to get it. That's what these A-Game strategies that I teach include. It's not like you have to be super human or even born extraordinary; anybody can apply it to themselves to change their lives.

If you want an A-Game high-quality guy, you need to get clear on how he will show up and how to spot him. Okay? Because I don't want you to get confused. We're talking about class. We're talking about a relationship-minded guy. You may meet a wealthy and successful guy, but it doesn't necessarily mean that he's bringing his A-Game to his relationships. He might bring his A-Game in business, but if he's not bringing his A-Game to love and dating, that's not what you're looking for either. Got it? Okay, so now I'm going to break it down for you, and we're going to talk about the A-Game man.

Keep in mind this is a brief overview here of what I go into at a much deeper level in my A-Game course. What an A-Game man is, and what an A-Game man isn't. First, we'll start with what is an A-Game man.

You can expect that an A-Game guy, who's operating at an A-Game level, is going to be very organized. And if you're not, that's a problem. You'll end up driving him nuts with your chaos. Right? This man is going to have his life in order. He is going to be on time. He's going to take charge of the situation. He is going to be accountable. You can count on this guy. He's always going to be, of course, very smart and a high achiever. But, he might not have ended up being the wealthiest guy on the planet. And of course, that's fine too.

And if he has interesting things to talk about and likes to do exciting things, that's an A-Game guy, ladies. That's whom you should always aspire to be with if you want an extraordinary life.

This A-Game guy is usually going to be very fit. This A-Game guy is going to have great style and great taste. If he's an A-Game guy who's looking for a serious, committed relationship, you're never going to have to question whether or not he's interested in you or whether he is playing around with you. This A-Game guy is reliable, and he's going to be clear on his intentions. He probably enjoys communication, and he's good at communicating.

An A-Game guy isn't going to be unsure of himself, what he wants, or be someone who jerks you around. You know those guys that that keep you guessing.

A guy that has you confused. You can't depend on a guy who cancels plans and only wants to waste your time and send too many text messages like a child. An A-Game man is a grown man who knows what he wants but keep in mind, and he won't put up with being jerked around either.

If at any point in time you feel like you're dating a man who is acting like a child, then that man is not an A-Game high-quality guy. Every man might be a bit of a pouty baby from time to time, no one is perfect, but an A-Game high-quality man will never be childish. You never have to worry about that. And a guy might look like he's high-quality (and let me be clear here) or that he's bringing his A-Game because there's a lot of men out there that can quickly look the part. Right? But don't be fooled.

He could look the part. He can be fit, good-looking, and put together. But there will always be telltale signs to look out for to show you that he isn't an A-Game man. If he seems like he's stuck in a rut, not talking about anything interesting, or he's not taking charge to ask you out on the interesting, exciting dates, this is not an A-Game high-quality guy. Here's another important thing for me to share with you. An A-Game high-quality guy that is seriously interested in a committed relationship with you is never going to rush you into bed. If he does, he's not an A-Game high-quality guy, or he's not seriously interested in you.

You only want to spend time with men who want to make plans with you. Who is interested in you, find out what you like doing, and make plans to see you. He is not texting you like a child and unsure of what he wants. If he doesn't know what he wants, and you're an A-Game woman, with your act together, then you'll spot that immediately, and you're not going to waste your time with that guy.

As you move through this process and become more of an A-Game woman, it's going to get easier to spot the guys who are A-Game men and the ones who aren't A-Game men. The ones who look high-quality, but they're not, and the ones that aren't A-Game at all. As you go through the process, it'll get easier to spot these guys, and you won't be willing or slightly interested in putting up with that unacceptable BS because now you're going to be bringing your A-Game. And you're only going to accept somebody who's at your level. You'll also start attracting these men much easier. Like attracts like.

And listen, telling someone to bring their A-Game is one thing, but it is harder than it sounds. I'll admit that. You don't know what you don't know. There are many facets and small details you have to implement in order to accurately bring your A-Game. I certainly didn't know about the A-Game until I saw it up close and personal while working with my billionaire and multi-millionaire clients. So it takes work; it takes goal setting and the willingness to be better today than you were yesterday.

CHAPTER 10

STRATEGY RECAP

Game On

OK—I hope you are excited to try something new to access the type of men you want to meet combined with newfound hope.

Are we clear?

1. Great men are on the dating apps.

Yes, the men you want to meet are there. Everyone is there these days, but you'll only really notice what your mind is focused on.

2. Mindset plays a huge part in the results you get.

If you remain stuck on a story (no good guys, men only want much younger, waste of time or he has to be right around your age), then you'll remain stuck in the same place a year from now as you are today.

3. You can't win if you don't stay in the game.

You cannot flip-flop. You must stay the course and be determined in your pursuit. Those who give up are the only ones that fail.

4. It's the dating Olympics.

You may not have connected with them before because you didn't realize you needed to treat it as though you were competing in the dating Olympics. Dating is competitive. Let's face it; everyone wants to be the one who takes home the prize. You have to bring it in every way and stand out from the crowd in the best way possible.

5. Optimize your profile to target the men you want to meet.

Don't get carried away with too many photos. Three is all you need, as long as they are really good photos of you, your face, and your body and represent you accurately. That is all a man needs to see to take action.

6. Dream BIG but also be realistic.

You understand you have to have a plan and not only know what you're looking for but BE what he's looking for too. The more perfect you want him to be, the more perfect you need to be as well.

7. Never accept crumbs from bums no matter how cute the guy looks.

Stop with the fantasy thinking that you can tame that bad boy, or if he gets to know you, then he'll make an effort. No, if he's not making an effort from the start, it will never get any better.

8. Swipe as the guys do and filter after.

You get exhausted with the dating apps because you waste too much time window shopping for the perfect guy. At this initial swiping phase, take it with a grain of salt. Have fun but don't give any of these guys a second thought until they demonstrate a real interest in you. Swiping on you means nothing. Detach and swipe away.

9. Set your standards out of the gate.

Only invest time into men who make an effort to let you know they are interested.

So if it is Bumble, wait until he extends the time; if it's Hinge, wait until he shows up and comments on your photo first, any of the other apps—it's ok to favorite him or 'like him,' but he has to make a move. And more than just Hi. You want a man that's curious and excited about you and never lower that bar.

10. Streamline a system: Match>Message>Call>Date

This all needs to happen within a few days. Compartmentalize. Maybe you only go on the apps for an hour each morning, and that's it. Make it a routine, but don't get sucked into swiping all throughout the day. Then a couple of good back and forth messages, and then either he or you (it's okay if it's you) needs to say, "Let's chat on a call." If he tries to text, route him back to getting on a call. This call is key to further pre-qualifying him to see if there is any chemistry, further interest, or red flags. Next step—I say a Zoom call. This is where you'll find out fast if it's worth investing the time to meet him in person. If you do these steps correctly, you will weed out the no effort men quickly so you end up only spending time dating better men.

Don't get too serious too quickly. Be playful, have fun. But also show him that you're smart, ask questions to find out if your lifestyles match, goals align and if there are genuinely shared common interests. And if not—NEXT.

11. If you want an A-Game man, you MUST bring your A-Game.

Water seeks its own level. You cannot get a man whom every woman wants unless you are an A-Game woman in every way, beyond looks.

Take Jessica, for example. I knew Jessica for years but only as a woman who filled out a profile in my database. We kept in touch, but to be honest, I bypassed her profile for several years because her photos were awful. I had no idea what she looked like because the pictures were small, blurry, and far away. I mean every mistake you could make, she was making. I know she was choosing photos her friends loved because they knew her and already loved her as a person. But I didn't know her, and I had never seen her in person. All I had to go on was her photos and the limited information she put on her profile. And yes, she did put down that she had a doctorate but didn't elaborate.

Here's the thing, if a woman's profile doesn't pop off the page, I move on because I review so many profiles I don't have time to waste (just like the men do on the dating apps). As a matchmaker, my job isn't to stop and take time to help women make better profiles, and they are required to figure that out on their own. I just review them and keep moving. And unfortunately, I have probably skipped over some fantastic women who might have been a match for my clients simply because the profile they filled out— didn't make them shine or stand out in any way.

That is why I decided to develop programs and write books designed to help women optimize everything they are doing when it comes to dating and even more so when it comes to attracting A-Game men.

So I hadn't talked to Jessica in a while when one day she emailed me some new photos. Not that these were much better but good enough that she got my attention. This woman in her early fifties had been hiding her six-pack abs and amazing body! Not to mention when I met her in person—holy moly. She was beautiful. Also, she was hiding the fact that she was a top ER doctor, and one of her passions was to work with Doctors Without Borders.

Ummmmm, ok, "Why were you hiding all of your greatness, lady?" I asked her this straight up. She said, "Well, I try not to let men know about my career or accomplishments because it seems to turn them off." Ok, I nodded, but I wasn't letting her off the hook that easily. So I asked, "And your pictures? What about those?"

She responded, "Well, I was in a hurry and uploaded what was handy."
Picture the emoji where there is a hand smacking your face that was me.

When I saw this woman (who was what most men wanted) struggling to meet great men, I knew I had to jump in and help. This is where it all started. Fixing her photos and amping up her profile was easy for me to do and for her a HUGE game changer. The other part we worked on was not as easy. She had fallen into a negative mindset.

She felt like the high-caliber men she wanted only wanted younger women. This is not true. Some do, but many would have fallen over themselves for her if she had better photos. Trust me! And if she was willing to let them know about her outstanding accomplishments, that would have catapulted her to the top of the heap. She would have seen better results and wouldn't have sunk into a mindset that was hard to reset.

If you're in a negative mindset, even if you are great in every other way, I still can't set you up with my clients. So we started working on resetting her beliefs about men. I encouraged her to follow my lead, be open-minded, give these guys a chance, and once her profile was shining bright, Jessica saw firsthand that the men she wanted were attracted to women her age. And she started dating up a storm! There were ups and downs as it is with dating, especially as you get older. Everyone has baggage, and we get pickier. Plus, the great options are fewer, so you will have ups and downs. It's normal, as I told her. So I held her up, kept her momentum going, and had her stick with it. But her mindset had already shifted as soon as she started getting the attention of the men she had wanted to meet.

Drum roll, please...

I am excited to say Miss Jessica met someone on a dating app who was what she wanted—handsome, smart, successful, and he was crazy about her. They even got married (similar to Audri's story) during the pandemic. And this, ladies, is why I do what I do.

I promise you will start to get different results if you follow what I've laid out for you here. Hopefully, you get better results. Doing it on your own is challenging, but it is doable for sure, and if you're up for it, you can even join my 60-day challenge.

I've been working with great guys and the type of men most women want for many years, so I know what it takes to make them sit up and take notice. But without me seeing firsthand every aspect of your profile, whom you're connecting with, and the messaging, it would be impossible for me to know why things aren't working out for you.

To learn more about the programs I offer, visit www.thegreatmanhunt.com.

Either way, I want you to find love and happiness with the best man possible. And I want you to know I am always here to help.

Xoxo

Gina

Printed in Great Britain
by Amazon